Sugar Inspirations

Pressure Piping

LESLEY HERBERT & SUE BALLARD

MEREHURST

Dedication

We dedicate this book to Tony H. and John B., our long-suffering husbands, and send our love to our children (Katie, Marc, John, Ruth, James and Joe), and to Tiana, born 5th January 1999.

First published 1999 by Merehurst Limited
Ferry House, 51–57 Lacy Road, Putney,
London SW15 1PR

Copyright © Merehurst Limited 1999
ISBN 1-85391-850-4

A catalogue record for this book is available from the British Library.

Commissioning Editor: Barbara Croxford
Editor: Helen Southall
Design: Anita Ruddell
Photography: Clive Streeter
Publishing Manager: Fia Fornari
Production Manager: Lucy Byrne
CEO & Publisher: Anne Wilson
International Sales Director: Kevin Lagden
UK Marketing & Sales Director:
Kathryn Harvey

Colour separation by Colourscan, Singapore
Printed in Hong Kong by Wing King Tong

Acknowledgements

The authors and publishers would like to thank the following manufacturers and suppliers:

Culpitt Cake Art
Culpitt Ltd
Jubilee Industrial Estate
Ashington
Northumberland
NE63 8UQ

Guy, Paul and Co. Ltd
Unit B4, Foundry Way
Little End Road
Eaton Socon
Cambs PE19 3JH

Orchard Products
51 Hallyburton Road
Hove
East Sussex BN3 7GP

PME Sugarcraft
Brember Road
South Harrow
Middlesex HA2 8UN

Renshaw Scott Ltd
Crown Street
Liverpool
L8 7RF

Squires Kitchen
Squires House
3 Waverley Lane
Farnham
Surrey
GU9 8BB

Tate & Lyle
Thames Refinery
Silvertown
London
E16 2EW

Twins
67–69 Victoria Road
Romford, Essex
RM1 2LT

Contents

Introduction

An original sugarcraft skill, pressure piping can be used in a wide variety of ways to great decorative effect.

The aim of this book is to demonstrate the wonderful versatility of pressure and figure piping with royal icing. This art form has long been an invaluable sugarcraft technique, and here it is brought to the fore in a stunning collection of original designs. The effects can be bold, novel, delicate or classic, and are suitable for a wide range of occasions.

Included on the following pages are clear, precise instructions for making numerous pictures or motifs (off-pieces) that can be added to a huge variety of cake designs. The colour photographs and helpful illustrations make the instructions easy to follow, so that all the designs are manageable by beginner and experienced cake decorator alike. Only basic equipment is needed; most cake decorators will already have a supply of piping tubes (tips) in their toolbox, and will be surprised to discover just what can be achieved by using royal icing and a variety of tubes.

We hope you will enjoy making some of the sugarcraft items and cakes featured in this book, or, if you prefer, that you will be able to use some of the templates and techniques to create your own designs.

Basic Recipe

All the designs and off-pieces in this book are made from royal icing, which is quick and simple to make by using the following recipe.

Royal Icing

Equipment must be thoroughly clean and free of grease, otherwise the icing will not hold the air which is beaten into it, making it heavy in consistency and unable to hold its shape. The ratio of ingredients for royal icing is six parts icing (confectioners') sugar to one part egg white.

Makes 220g (7oz)
30g (1oz/6 teaspoons) egg white (at room temperature)
185g (6oz/1 cup) icing (confectioners') sugar

1 Place the egg white in a bowl with three-quarters of the icing sugar. Beat on slow speed for 2 minutes, using an electric beater.

2 Adjust the consistency by adding the remaining icing sugar, and continue to beat on slow speed until the icing is of full peak consistency (page 5).

3 Cover the icing with a polythene bag and a damp cloth to prevent the surface from drying and forming a crust.

Tips

If using egg white (albumen) powder (pure or substitute), reconstitute it in the proportions of 90g (3oz/½ cup) to 625 ml (1 pint/2½ cups) water.

Egg whites are measured by weight rather than by number. This method gives accurate results, particularly when making royal icing.

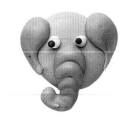

4

Techniques

Royal Icing Consistencies

Full Peak For full peak consistency, you need to use freshly beaten royal icing. Full peak icing should have a good shine, and when the beater is lifted out, the icing should form a peak that holds its shape.

Soft Peak Reduce freshly beaten icing by 'buttering it down'. To do this, place the icing on a flat, clean, grease-free surface and spread it backwards and forwards with a palette knife until it is of the required consistency. This action will remove some of the air bubbles and make the icing smoother and softer. The tip of the peak should flop over.

Pressure Piping Consistency Butter the icing down as for soft peak and gradually reduce the consistency with water or egg white until the icing still holds its shape but goes smooth if a knife is agitated on the surface.

Run-out Consistency Reduce fresh full peak icing using water or egg white until it is thin enough to very slowly find its own level again after a knife has been drawn through it. The royal icing should be kept as stiff as is practicable; if it is reduced too much, the run-out might not set with enough strength.

Basic Pressure Piping Shapes

The following basic shapes (illustrated on page 6) are used to create many of the designs in this book. Use soft peak icing.

Bulb Holding the piping bag at a 90° angle, with the tube (tip) just above (not touching) the piping surface, squeeze the bag with even pressure to form a dome (circle) of icing. Release the pressure and take off gently. If small peaks occur, they can be touched down using a damp artists' paintbrush. Large peaks can be caused if you squeeze the piping bag while lifting the piping tube from the bulb. Holding the piping tube too near the piping surface can cause badly shaped bulbs.

Shell Holding the piping bag at a 45° angle, squeeze the bag to produce a bulb of icing. Gradually reducing the pressure, sweep the tube down towards the piping surface to form the tail of the shell. To produce an eye indent, push the tube firmly into the bulb of icing and drag the icing out.

Shells with Indents These shapes are ideal for forming ears. By increasing or decreasing the pressure applied to the piping bag as the tube is removed from the shell shape can alter the indent of the ear.

'C' Scroll To form a 'C' scroll, hold the piping tube at a 90° angle and pipe a bulb of icing, applying gentle pressure and twisting and turning your wrist to create a 'C' shape. To create texture in the 'C' scroll, gently agitate the piping tube up and down while releasing the pressure on the piping bag. If the icing does not hold the texture, it may be because the icing is too soft, or because the piping bag has been agitated too quickly, causing the surface tension to collapse.

'S' Scroll Hold the piping bag at a 90° angle and squeeze a bulb of icing on to the icing surface. Apply slightly more pressure whilst agitating the bag up and down to form the beginning of the scroll. Gently releasing the pressure, form the 'S' shape by turning your wrist clockwise and then anti-clockwise. It is helpful to visualise the shape as you are piping.

'C' Shape Holding the piping bag at a 90° angle, pipe a curved 'C' shape using constant, even pressure. Release the pressure on the bag and remove the piping tube with a backward motion to help prevent a peak forming.

Rope Hold the piping bag at a 45° angle. Using constant pressure, rotate the bag of icing, gradually moving your hand across the icing surface to create a coil effect.

Zigzag Hold the piping bag at a 60° angle. Using constant pressure, with the piping tube touching the piping surface, pipe a zigzag line of icing. This can be piped straight or in various shapes, such as leaves.

Pressure Piping Motifs

The designs in this book are decorated with pressure piped run-out pieces and motifs. The following basic hints will help make your off-pieces a success. For detailed instructions, see page 19.

1 Before piping, always grease the cellophane or waxed paper very lightly with white vegetable fat (shortening). Once thoroughly dry, remove the pressure piping by sliding a cranked palette knife gently underneath it to separate it from the cellophane.

2 Drying time varies, depending on the size of the motif and the temperature and humidity in the room. Small pieces will dry within an hour if placed under a warm lamp; larger pieces, such as the bears on page 41, are best left overnight.

3 To use the templates in this book, first trace or photocopy them from the page, then transfer to thin card, and cut out if necessary. To make motifs in reverse, turn the tracing paper over and use that as your template.

Pressure Piping Birds

Birds make an attractive decoration and are simply piped using basic pressure piping shapes.

Hovering Bird

1 Secure a piece of cellophane or waxed paper over the wings template (right) and pressure pipe the front wing using a no. 1 piping tube (tip) and soft peak royal icing.

2 Beginning at the base of the wing, pipe a loop of icing, gradually increasing the pressure to the outside of the loop and releasing the pressure as you return to the base. Continue piping loops to form a fan-shaped wing. (On some birds a second layer of icing is piped to give a feather effect.) Allow the icing to dry.

3 Secure a piece of cellophane or waxed paper over the bird template and pipe the back wing and tail as before.

4 For the bird's head and body, change to pressure piping consistency icing and a no. 1 piping tube. For the head, pipe a bulb of icing, forming the beak as you remove the piping tube.

5 Agitating the icing and keeping the pressure even, pipe the body, following the shape of the template. Use a damp artists' paintbrush to reduce any take-off mark. Allow to dry.

6 Using soft peak icing, attach the wings. Support, if necessary, with tissue paper until dry.

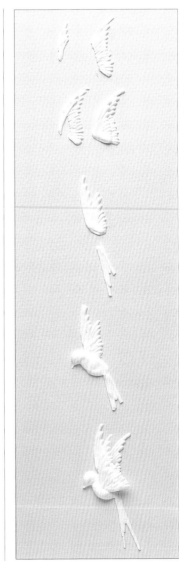

Stork

1 Secure a piece of cellophane or waxed paper over the template on page 9.

2 First pressure pipe the wing as described on page 7, using a no. 1 piping tube (tip) and soft peak royal icing. Leave to dry.

3 Secure another piece of cellophane or waxed paper over the template and pipe an 'S' scroll to form the head and neck, using a no. 2 tube and soft peak icing. The beak is formed by piping two lines from the head, overlapping at the tip, using a no. 1 piping tube and soft peak royal icing.

4 To pipe the legs, use a no. 2 piping tube and pipe lines, pausing halfway to form the knee joints.

5 Change to a no. 3 piping tube and full peak royal icing, and pipe a large 'C' scroll to form the body. Attach the wing while the icing is still soft.

Three-dimensional Sitting Bird

1 Secure a piece of cellophane or waxed paper over the left and right wings templates on page 9, and pressure pipe the wings as described on page 7. Leave to dry.

2 Fold a piece of cellophane to form a 90° angle. Using a no. 1 piping tube (tip) and soft peak royal icing, pressure pipe the tail on the vertical side of the fold. The tail is piped in three small shells.

3 Using a no. 2 piping tube and full peak royal icing, pipe a bulb to form the body on the horizontal side of the folded cellophane. Pipe a small bulb on top to form the head, pulling the tube out of the icing to form the beak.

4 Attach the wings using a no. 1 piping tube and soft peak royal icing while the body is still soft.

8

Blue Birds and Doves

Use the templates on this page to pressure pipe blue birds and doves following the instructions on pages 7 and 8. Instructions for making the ducks are on page 13.

Stork

Small Bird (page 10)

Blue Birds (page 19)

Dove

Three-dimensional Sitting Bird

Christening Cake

This simple design is adorned with pressure piped decorations.

Materials

25cm (10 inch) round rich fruit cake
38cm (15 inch) petal-shaped cake board
1.25kg (2½lb) almond paste (marzipan)
1.75kg (3½lb) sugarpaste (rolled fondant)
185g (6oz) royal icing
Apricot glaze
Blue liquid food colouring
Pale blue dusting powder (petal dust/blossom tint)
White fat (shortening) for greasing
Lemon satin ribbon for bow

Equipment

Cellophane or waxed paper
Nos. 0, 1 and 2 piping tubes (tips)
Piping bags
Airbrush (optional)
Tracing paper
Soft dusting brush
Fine artists' paintbrush

Decorations

9 pairs yellow bootees (page 15)
6 pale blue half sleighs (page 28)
18 swans (page 14)

Preparation

1 Brush the cake with apricot glaze, coat with almond paste and leave to dry for three days. Coat the cake and board separately with sugarpaste, and leave to dry for three days. Attach the cake to the centre of the board with a small amount of royal icing.

2 Pressure pipe one small bird following the instructions on page 7 (templates on page 9). Leave to dry.

Cake top

3 Lightly grease a piece of cellophane with white fat and secure over the 'Baby' template on page 47. Using a no. 2 piping tube, pressure pipe small shells in white or blue soft peak royal icing to form the lettering, applying more pressure on the bag where the strokes are thicker. Allow to dry. If you have used white icing, airbrush or dust blue when dry.

4 Trace the bib template on page 47 on to a piece of paper large enough to cover the top of the cake. Cut the bib shape out of the centre and lay the remaining border over the cake top. Using blue petal dust or the airbrush, colour the central area by dusting from the template on to the cake, leaving the centre of the bib paler.

of the bib, and a lemon ribbon bow to the top of the bib.

Cake sides

8 Pipe a small shell border around the base of the cake using a no. 2 piping tube and soft peak white royal icing.

9 Using pale blue liquid food colouring and a fine paint-brush, paint marks on the board around the base of the cake to represent water.

10 Positioning a sleigh towards the right of each petal of the cake board, secure each one to the side of the cake using a no. 1 piping tube and soft peak icing. Attach three swans in front of each sleigh. To represent reins, pipe drop loops of full peak blue icing from swan to swan, and to the sleigh, using a no. 1 piping tube.

5 Pipe a picot edge to the bib using a no. 0 icing tube and soft peak icing.

6 Carefully lift the lettering from the cellophane and secure on top of the cake with dots of icing. Attach the small piped bird to the letter 'B'.

7 Attach the yellow bootees in pairs at each petal point

Christening Motifs

These attractive off-pieces can be used as alternative decorations for the Christening Cake (page 10) or for the decorated chocolate eggs on page 16.

Duck and Duckling

1 Secure a piece of lightly greased cellophane or waxed paper over the duck templates (right). Using a no. 1 piping tube (tip) and soft peak white royal icing, pressure pipe shells to form the wing. Leave to dry.

2 Secure another piece of cellophane over the templates and, with a no. 1 tube and soft peak egg yellow royal icing, pipe the beak and feet.

3 Using a no. 2 piping tube and pressure piping consistency white royal icing, pipe an

'S' scroll to form the head and neck. Squeeze very hard on the piping bag and agitate the icing to form the body. Agitating the icing will help create a smooth shiny surface. Set the wing into the body before the icing dries. Pipe a blue dot for the eye.

4 The duckling is piped in the same way.

Stork with Baby

1 Secure a piece of lightly greased cellophane or waxed paper over the template below.

2 Using a no.1 piping tube (tip) and soft peak royal icing, pressure pipe long shells to form the wing. Allow to dry.

3 Secure another piece of cellophane over the template. Using a no. 1 piping tube and soft peak paprika or flesh royal icing, pipe the back leg and foot. The foot is formed by piping three shells. Agitate the icing to pipe the leg. Using the same icing, pipe the front leg, following the template. Pipe a bulb for the baby's head.

4 Change to a no. 2 piping tube and soft peak white icing, and pipe an 'S' scroll for the head and neck. Agitating the piping tube, pipe a large shell to form the body. The shawl around the baby and the bow on the stork's beak are formed by piping shells.

5 Change to a petal piping tube and black icing, and pipe the stork's hat by holding the tube flat against the head and piping a line. The peak is piped with a shell movement.

6 Return to paprika or flesh icing and pipe two lines to form the beak.

7 Remove the wing from the cellophane and attach it to the body while the icing is still soft. Allow to dry.

8 Using an artists' fine paintbrush and black food colouring, paint dots for the stork's and baby's eyes.

Swan

1 Secure a lightly greased piece of cellophane or waxed paper over the template (above right).

2 Using a no. 1 piping tube (tip) and soft peak white royal icing, pipe a set of wings. Set aside to dry. Using the same tube, pipe the back tail feathers on to another piece of cellophane.

3 Change to a no. 2 piping tube and pressure piping consistency royal icing, and pipe an 'S' scroll for the head and neck. Apply more pressure and pipe a large shell for the body. Change back to a no. 1 tube and push the tube into the head

(while the icing is still soft) and pull out a beak shape. Pipe a small scroll for the back leg. Allow to dry.

4 When completely dry, turn the body over and repeat on the reverse side.

5 Stand the swan up, using a small bulb of royal icing to secure. Attach the wings with full peak royal icing, supporting with tissue paper until dry if necessary. Paint a black eye on each side using an artists' fine paintbrush and black food colouring.

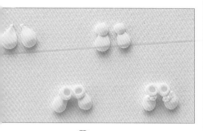

Bootees

1 Secure a piece of lightly greased cellophane or waxed paper over the template (above right).

2 Using a no. 1 piping tube (tip) and soft peak lemon royal icing, pipe a shell to form the foot of the bootee. Pipe a bulb of the same icing over the tail of the shell to form the heel. Pipe three circles of icing around the edge of the bulb to form a coil of icing. Allow to dry.

3 Using a no. 0 piping tube and soft peak white royal icing, pipe two loops with a dot in the middle to form a bow.

4 Repeat to make a pair of bootees.

Rattle with Ribbon

1 Secure a piece of lightly greased cellophane or waxed paper over the template below.

2 Using a no. 2 piping tube (tip) and pressure piping consistency yellow royal icing, pipe a long shell shape for the handle. Pipe two bulbs of icing, the second slightly larger than the first, at the thin end. Brush the icing out at the edge to help give the rattle strength. Pipe a large bulb to form the rattle. Allow to dry.

3 With a no. 0 piping tube and pressure piping consistency white royal icing, pipe two decorative lines across the bulb and small shells to form a heart motif.

4 To make the bow, secure a piece of cellophane or waxed paper over the template (below left). Pipe the bow using soft peak white royal icing and a no. 1 piping tube. Allow to dry before attaching to the rattle with a small dot of icing.

Variation

For a simpler rattle, pipe a loop of yellow royal icing for the handle and a smaller bulb for the rattle, using the template (right). Decorate with dots of different sizes.

Welcome Baby Egg

These attractive chocolate eggs are decorated using off-pieces
and pressure piping directly on to the chocolate surface.

Materials

23cm (9 inch) white chocolate
egg
Oval white chocolate base
250g (8oz) royal icing
Pale pink, green and cream food
colourings
750g (1½lb) white chocolate,
melted

Equipment

Cellophane or waxed paper
Small ribbon piping tube (tip)
Tracing paper
Scriber
Nos. 1 and 11 piping tubes (tips)

Decorations

1 stork with baby (page 14)
3 flying blue birds (page 9)
9 forget-me-nots (page 22)

1 Pipe four loops for the
bow on to a piece of lightly
greased cellophane or waxed
paper using a small ribbon piping tube and soft peak pale pink
royal icing. Allow to dry.

2 Trace the inscription on
page 18 and scribe on to
the surface of one half of the
egg. Pipe the letters using a no.
1 piping tube and soft peak
pale pink royal icing, using
simple lines with a rope effect
in places.

3 Stick the halves of the
egg together and then
secure to the base using melted
white chocolate.

4 Using a no. 1 piping tube
and soft peak green royal
icing, pipe small groups of lines
for grass. Attach the stork using
soft peak royal icing.

5 Pipe the tails of the bow
directly on to the egg
using the small ribbon piping
tube and soft peak pale pink
royal icing. Attach the bow loops
to the top centre of the egg.

6 Place the blue birds and
forget-me-nots in position
and secure with soft peak royal
icing.

7 Using a no. 11 piping
tube and full peak cream
royal icing, pipe a large
shell border around the
edge of the egg.

Variations
Traditional Easter Egg

Scribe the inscription on page
18 on to a milk chocolate egg
and pipe using a no. 1 piping
tube (tip) and soft peak egg yellow royal icing. Form the letters
by piping small shells. Pipe
stems and leaves on the egg
using a leaf piping bag (page 25)
and soft peak green royal icing.
Attach groups of narcissi (page
21) and violets (page 22). Add
an Easter bunny made using the
template on page 18 and following the techniques on page 19.
Pipe a shell border as in
step 7,
above.

16

leaves (after trimming the bag a little larger, if necessary). Secure pink roses, half roses and rose buds (page 23) using bulbs of full peak royal icing. Pipe green calyxes on the rose buds using the leaf piping bag. Pipe a shell border as in step 7 on page 16.

Basket of Flowers Egg

A flat-sided egg is used for this design, but a rounded egg would also be suitable. Using a 50:50 mixture of sugarpaste (rolled fondant) and pastillage, create a piece of triangular padding for the inside of the basket, using the template below as a guide. Secure the padding to the egg with soft peak royal icing.

Colour some of the same 50:50 mixture cream and roll out on a non-stick board. Mark a diamond pattern on the paste with the pointed end of a veining tool, then cut out the basket shape, using the template below. Dampen the padding with water

Rose Easter Egg

If liked, pipe an inscription on to a dark chocolate egg, using the template below for guidance, if necessary. Use a no. 1 piping tube and soft peak white royal icing. Embellish by piping small scroll shapes around the inscription. Using a leaf piping bag (page 25), pipe stems in a large 'C' shape, then pipe some

or sugar glue and attach the basket piece. Cut a strip of paste for a handle and texture with a ball tool.

Using a small leaf bag (page 25), pipe leaves directly on to the egg. Attach 8 full pale peach roses (page 23), 4 rose buds and forget-me-nots (page 22) in a decorative design. Pipe a shell border as in step 7 on page 16.

Springtime Motifs

The decorations on these pages have a springtime or Easter theme, but could be used on any children's (or adults') cakes.

Techniques

Before pressure piping each motif, look at the illustration and template carefully and decide which parts of it appear the furthest away from you. Always pressure pipe these areas first, then gradually build up the motif, allowing each area to dry before adding the next. Increase the pressure on the piping bag in areas where a three-dimensional effect is needed.

Blue Birds

Follow the instructions for piping birds on pages 7–9 to make the two blue birds (templates on page 9). The ring of hearts is made by piping a double circle of linked shells, following the template above.

Chicks with Eggs

Use the template to create either of the designs, then decorate with violets or narcissi (pages 22 and 21) and pressure piped leaves (page 25).

Birds on a Branch

First pressure pipe the branches, then the birds, following the instructions on pages 7–9 and using the template above. Add leaves (page 25) and forget-me-nots (page 22) as desired.

Chicks in the Nest

Pressure pipe the branch and leaves (page 25), then add the nest and chicks (template above). Paint on dots for the chicks' eyes.

Decorative Borders

These borders, made by pressure piping the same design repeatedly, make a very attractive finish to the side of an Easter, Christening or small child's birthday cake.

Pressure Piping Flowers

Many simple flowers can be made using the same pressure piping technique.

Piping Petals

1 Many makes and varieties of petal piping tube (tip) are available, for both left- and right-handed users. The size of the tube selected will determine the size of the completed flower.

2 To form a petal shape, the icing must be stiff and well beaten. Piping bags need to be strong so we suggest making them from double greaseproof paper.

3 Cut small squares of waxed paper. Pipe a small dot of icing on to a flower nail to secure a square of paper.

4 Position the piping bag so the widest end of the tube

is in the centre of the square of paper, with the narrow edge towards the outside. The curved side of the tube should be facing up.

5 Attach the icing to the paper, then squeeze and lift the tube slightly as you turn the flower nail, thus creating a horseshoe shape. Stop squeezing and take the tube away.

6 Repeat to make as many petals as required to complete the flower.

Daisy

1 With a no. 1 piping tube (tip) and pressure piping consistency egg yellow royal icing, pressure pipe several small bulbs on to waxed paper. While the icing is still soft, dredge with yellow pollen. Shake off the excess and allow to dry.

2 Using well beaten full peak royal icing and a petal piping tube, pipe a ring of five petals following the instructions above. Tuck each petal behind the previous one as you begin to pipe.

3 While the icing is still soft, place a yellow bulb in the centre of each flower.

Narcissus

1 Using well beaten full peak white royal icing and a petal piping tube (tip), pressure pipe a ring of six petals following the instructions above.

Tuck each petal behind the previous one as you begin to pipe.

2 Before the petals are dry, pipe three rings, using a no. 1 tube and soft peak yellow royal icing, to form a coil for the trumpet in the centre.

Violet

1 Using well beaten full peak violet royal icing and a small petal piping tube (tip), pressure pipe the bottom petal first, following the instructions on page 21. (This forms one-third of the completed flower.) Pipe the petal in a fan shape, using a small zigzag movement to create texture.

2 Pipe two long, thin, overlapping petals opposite the fan-shaped petal. Finally, pipe two plain petals in the gaps on either side of the fan-shaped petal.

3 Using a no. 0 piping tube and soft peak yellow royal icing, pipe a small shell in the centre of the flower.

Pansy

1 Pansies are piped using the same method as violets but you will require two petal piping tubes (tips) of the same size.

2 Fill one piping bag fitted with a petal piping tube with full peak yellow royal icing, and the second with two different colours of icing. Fill them so that yellow icing comes out of the narrow edge of the tube and violet icing comes out of the

wide part of the tube, thus creating a two-tone effect (see Notes below).

3 Pipe in the same way as violets, using two-tone icing to create a realistic pansy.

Forget-me-not

1 On a sheet of waxed paper, pressure pipe a dot for the centre of the flower, using a no. 1 piping tube (tip) and soft peak yellow royal icing.

2 Using a no. 1 piping tube and soft peak blue icing, pipe a ring of five dots around the yellow centre.

Notes

The consistency of icing used for the forget-me-not is very important. If the icing is too stiff it will be difficult to pipe dots without peaks; if it is too soft, the dots will lose their shape and run together.

To fill a bag with two colours of icing, place one colour in one side of the bag and the second colour in the other side. Flatten the bag and squeeze until both colours can be piped together.

Pressure Piping Roses

Full roses, half-open roses and rose buds make beautiful cake decorations,
and can be made in a variety of colours.

Large Pink Rose

1 Attach a cone of almond paste (marzipan) to a cocktail stick (toothpick).

2 Colour well-beaten full peak royal icing pink and use to fill a large greaseproof paper piping bag fitted with a large petal piping tube (tip).

3 Hold the cocktail stick so you can rotate it between the thumb and finger of one hand. Hold the piping bag so that the thin end of the tube is facing upwards at a 45° angle and the curved side of the tube is facing the almond paste cone. Squeeze the bag and attach the icing to the top of the cone. Continue to squeeze the bag while rotating the cocktail stick to form the rose centre. Release pressure and take off the tube.

4 For an open rose, turn the tube so that the curve faces away from the almond paste, but always with the thin edge of the tube uppermost. Squeeze the bag again and attach the icing to the almond paste just below the piped rose centre. Continue squeezing with even pressure while turning the

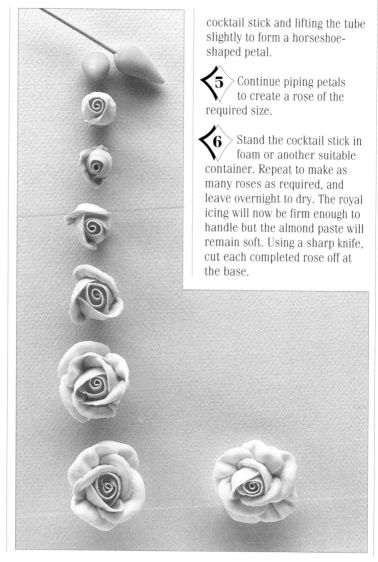

cocktail stick and lifting the tube slightly to form a horseshoe-shaped petal.

5 Continue piping petals to create a rose of the required size.

6 Stand the cocktail stick in foam or another suitable container. Repeat to make as many roses as required, and leave overnight to dry. The royal icing will now be firm enough to handle but the almond paste will remain soft. Using a sharp knife, cut each completed rose off at the base.

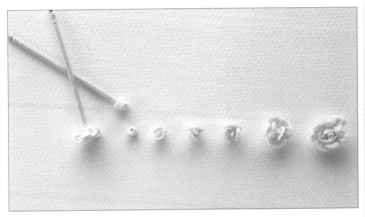

Small Rose

1 Following the same method as for a large rose (page 23), pipe small roses directly on to cocktail sticks (toothpicks), omitting the almond paste (marzipan).

2 Thread a square of waxed paper on to the bottom of each cocktail stick and slide the paper up to remove the completed rose. Leave to dry.

Miniature Rose

Follow the technique for small roses, above, but use a no. 2 plain piping tube, flattened on one side with a pair of pliers, instead of a petal tube.

Rose Bud

1 If appropriate, select a petal piping tube (tip) that will produce buds of the size you require alongside the full version of the rose.

2 Holding the piping bag at a 90° angle, with the thin edge of the tube uppermost, squeeze the bag and pipe a shell on to a sheet of cellophane or waxed paper. Working from the right-hand side, squeeze the bag and lift the tube up and over the shell to form the first petal, keeping the pressure even.

3 Tuck the tube into the left-hand side of the shell and pipe a second petal in the same way. Stop squeezing the piping bag and remove the tube as you would if piping a shell. Continue to add petals each side of the flower until the bud is large enough for your requirements.

Notes

1 This method gives another dimension to a spray of flowers because the bud has a flat side and can be used in many ways to enhance your display.

2 A calyx can be piped with a leaf bag (page 25) once the rose bud is in its required position (as on the Rose Easter Egg on page 18).

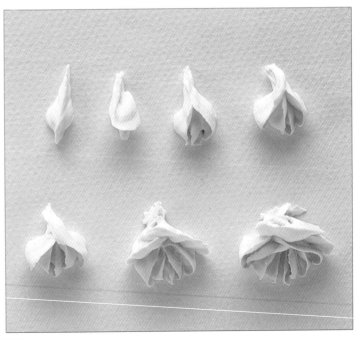

Pressure Piping Leaves

Leaves are ideal for filling gaps or finishing off floral displays on cakes or other decorated pieces.

Making a Leaf Bag

1 Half fill a small grease-proof paper piping bag with full peak green royal icing. Fold the top of the bag over so the icing is squeezed down the bag.

2 Flatten the point of the piping bag and cut into a small 'V' shape with scissors.

Small Leaves

1 Using a no. 1 or 2 piping tube (tip) and full peak green royal icing, pressure pipe small shell shapes directly on to the piping surface alongside piped forget-me-nots, miniature roses or any other small flowers.

2 Using a leaf piping bag (see above) and full peak royal icing, hold the bag at a 45° angle and squeeze the piping bag to produce leaf shapes. Take off as for shells.

Large Leaves

1 Prepare a leaf piping bag, as above, but cut an inverted 'V' into the point. This will put a centre vein down each leaf and help to achieve a nice point at the end of each leaf.

2 Agitate the icing with the piping tube, as you pipe, to give the leaf more texture and shape.

Holly

1 Using a no. 1 piping tube (tip) and soft peak green royal icing, pipe a zigzag leaf shape on waxed paper.

2 With a dampened fine artists' paintbrush, pull out points down each side of the leaf.

3 Finally, bring the brush through the centre of the leaf from tip to stem to create a centre vein.

4 Repeat to make as many leaves as required. Once the leaves are in position, pressure pipe berries between pairs of them with a no. 1 piping tube and soft peak red royal icing.

Christmas Sleigh Cake

This traditional cake is decorated with classic images of Christmas: a sleigh drawn by reindeer, holly, bells and candles. For some alternative motifs, see page 30.

Materials

30x25cm (12x10 inch) oval rich fruit cake
38x33cm (15x13 inch) oval cake board
1.5kg (3lb) almond paste (marzipan)
2kg (4lb) white sugarpaste (rolled fondant)
Apricot glaze
30g (1oz) pastillage
Small quantity of royal icing
Caster (superfine) sugar
Red food colouring
Edible gold lustre powder
Edible silver snowflake

Equipment

Tracing paper
Scriber
Piping bags
Nos. 1 and 2 piping tubes (tips)
Thin card
Craft knife or scalpel
Artists' paintbrushes

Decorations

65 holly leaves (page 25)
24 small holly leaves
4 candles (page 29)
4 bells (page 29)
4 candy canes (page 29)
1 sleigh (page 28)
9 reindeer (page 28)

Preparation

1 Brush the cake with apricot glaze, coat with almond paste, and leave to dry for three days. Coat the cake and board separately with sugarpaste, and leave to dry for three days. Attach the cake to the board with royal icing.

Cake top

2 Trace the oval template on pages 46–47 and scribe on to the top of the cake. Using a no. 2 piping tube and run-out consistency white royal icing, pressure pipe a thick line along the scribed oval, leaving a gap. While still wet, dredge with caster sugar to create a snow effect.

3 Pressure pipe the ribbon on the cake top using a no. 1 piping tube and pressure piping consistency red royal icing. Use a zigzag motion to create texture. Leave to dry.

4 Attach holly leaves along the ribbon with small dots of royal icing. Add holly berries as described on page 25.

Cake side

5 Cut a strip of greaseproof paper as wide as the height of the cake and as long as the circumference. Divide the strip into 12 equal sections, marking each section with a fold. Draw a straight line 6cm (2½ inches) up from the bottom edge of the strip. Cut scallops between the section folds in the bottom edge.

6 Place the paper template around the cake and make a pin mark in the sugarpaste at each point where the drawn line crosses a fold. Scribe the scallop pattern around the base.

7 Trace the side plaque template on page 47, transfer to thin card and cut out. Roll out the pastillage quite thinly on a non-stick board and cut out 12 side plaques, using the card template. Dust with edible gold lustre powder, and attach to the cake side using water before they are dry, placing the point of each plaque at a pin mark.

8 Using a no. 2 piping tube and full peak white royal icing, pipe a zigzag line around the scribed scallop line.

9 Using full peak red royal icing, drop a loop over each zigzag scallop and around the base of each plaque.

Decorations

10 Attach the candles, bells and candy canes to the plaques around the cake. Add small holly leaves and berries to each one. Pipe three red dots at the point of each plaque.

11 Place the completed sleigh on top of the cake, securing with a no. 1 piping tube and soft peak white royal icing. Attach the reindeer by piping small dots of icing on the feet and placing on top of the cake. Pipe drop loops between the reindeer and to the sleigh to represent reins.

12 Dab small amounts of royal icing around the sleigh and reindeer, and brush with edible silver snowflake to give a glistening snow effect.

Sleigh

1 Trace the templates on page 47, transfer to thin card and cut out.

2 Colour a small amount of pastillage red. Roll out the pastillage quite thinly on a non-stick board. Using a craft knife, cut out a right and left side of the sleigh, and a back, front and base. Leave to dry on a flat surface, turning the pieces after about 2 hours to aid even drying and prevent sticking. Leave for 24 hours to dry completely.

3 With a no. 1 piping tube (tip) and soft peak white royal icing, pressure pipe the decorations on the sides of the sleigh, using the template as a guide. Leave to dry.

4 Secure a piece of lightly greased cellophane or waxed paper over the sleigh template and pressure pipe 'Y' shapes to form the blade supports, using a no. 2 piping tube and soft peak white icing. Carefully position the sides of the sleigh on to the tails of the 'Y' shapes while the icing is still wet. Pressure pipe the scroll design for the base blades of the sleigh and leave to dry.

5 Soften some red pastillage to a piping consistency with water and put into a piping bag (no tube required). Glue the front, back and base to one side of the sleigh, then stand it up to balance it before attaching the other side. Leave to dry.

Reindeer

1 Secure a piece of lightly greased cellophane or waxed paper over the template below. Using a no. 0 piping tube (tip) and full peak white or pale brown royal icing, pressure pipe the antlers and ear.

2 Change to a no. 1 tube and pressure piping consistency icing and pressure pipe a bulb for the nose. Pipe the back front leg, applying slightly more pressure at the knee and hoof. Pipe the second front leg, again with extra pressure at the knee and hoof.

3 Pipe the neck and body, agitating the icing slightly with the tube to help achieve a smooth finish.

4 Pipe the back legs as for the front legs, tucking the tube into the soft icing of the body to begin. Finally, pipe a bulb for the tail. Leave to dry.

5 If you have used white icing, airbrush the reindeer brown when dry.

Note

To create a double row of reindeer to pull the sleigh, as on the Christmas Sleigh Cake (page 26), you will need to pipe some in reverse. To do this, trace the reindeer template, then turn the paper over and use this as your template.

Bell

1 Using a no. 2 piping tube (tip) and soft peak white royal icing, and holding the piping bag at a 90° angle, pressure pipe a large bulb on to a sheet of waxed paper. Lift the bag slightly and pipe a second bulb, a little smaller, directly on top of the first. Lift the piping bag again and pipe a small third bulb directly on top of the second. Leave to dry for about 1 hour,

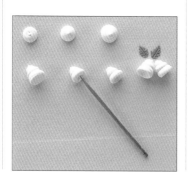

until the outside of the bell is quite firm but the inside is still quite soft.

2 Remove the soft icing with a cocktail stick (toothpick) to create a hollow bell. (Should the bell break, allow the icing longer to dry next time, but take care not to allow the bell to dry completely before removing the icing from inside.)

3 Using a no. 1 piping tube and full peak white royal icing, pipe a line and a dot for the clanger in the bell.

Candles

1 Secure a piece of cellophane or waxed paper over the template below. With a no. 1 piping tube (tip) and soft peak red royal icing, pressure pipe the candles in lines to create texture. Leave to dry.

2 Place some full peak yellow and orange royal icing in a small piping bag (page

22) and cut as for a leaf bag (page 25). Pressure pipe a small 'leaf' on top of each candle to represent a flame.

Candy Cane

1 Secure a piece of lightly greased cellophane or waxed paper over the template below. Using a no. 1 or no. 2 piping tube (tip), depending on the size required, fill a bag with soft peak red and white royal icing (page 22).

2 The cane is piped in two sections so that you are always piping towards yourself, giving a more accurate finish. Using a zigzag movement, pressure pipe the top of the cane first, then break off and turn the template and paper. Attach the icing again and pipe the remainder of the cane. Leave to dry.

Christmas Motifs

These seasonal motifs can be used as alternative side decorations on the Christmas Sleigh Cake (page 26) or on any Christmas cake of your own design.

Rudolph

1 Secure a piece of lightly greased cellophane or waxed paper over the template (right). Using a no. 1 piping tube (tip) and full peak brown royal icing, pipe the antlers.

2 Fill a small piping bag fitted with a small petal piping tube with soft peak white and brown royal icing (with the white icing to the thin edge of the tube). Pressure pipe two petal shapes (page 21) for ears.

3 Using a no. 3 tube and pressure piping consis-tency brown royal icing, pressure pipe the head. Squeeze the bag firmly to form a large teardrop for the face, using the template as a guide, and agitat-ing the icing with the tube to help create a smooth surface. Remove the tube at the nose position. Leave to dry under a warm lamp for about 1 hour.

4 With a no. 1 tube and pressure piping consis-tency white royal icing, pressure pipe two shells for the eyes. Using a no. 2 tube and pressure piping consistency red icing, pipe a bulb for the nose. Allow to dry.

5 Finally, paint in the eyes and mouth using a fine artists' paintbrush and black food colouring.

Santa Claus

1 Secure a piece of cello-phane or waxed paper over the template on page 31. Colour small amounts of full peak royal icing red, black and flesh.

2 Using a no. 1 piping tube (tip) and soft peak black icing, pressure pipe Santa's boots, starting with a bulb for the foot area, then filling in to cover the boot area on the tem-plate, increasing pressure on the bag to give relief to the legs.

3 Using a no. 1 piping tube and soft peak red icing, pressure pipe the legs, using the template as a guide and adding pressure at the knee area.

4 With soft peak flesh icing, and a no. 1 piping tube, pressure pipe the face, agitating the icing with the tube to create a smooth surface. Add features to the face: two shells for cheeks, a small bulb for the nose, and a bulb on each side for the ears.

5 Using a no. 1 piping tube and soft peak red royal icing, pressure pipe the body, increasing the pressure where necessary to give it shape. Pipe the arms with the same red

icing, adding pressure to give shape to the elbows.

6 Pipe the gloves using black icing: one large shell for each fist and one small shell for each thumb. Pipe the hat with a no. 1 tube and soft peak red icing. Pipe the top of the hat to match the template, and add a small scroll for the end.

7 Using a no. 1 piping tube and full peak white icing, pipe the fur around the bottom of Santa's coat, using a zigzag motion to give texture. Pipe the fur around the wrists, then pipe the beard, forming small shells upwards towards the mouth.

8 Pipe the fur around Santa's hat and the bobble on the end. Pipe Santa's eyebrows and moustache.

9 For the eyes, pipe two small bulbs of soft peak icing with a no. 1 tube, then fin-

ish with tiny bulbs of black icing for the pupils. Finally, pipe the belt with black icing and the buckle with white.

Christmas Tree

1 Secure a piece of lightly greased cellophane or waxed paper over the template below.

2 Using a no. 1 piping tube (tip) and full peak brown royal icing, pipe the tree shape, using a zigzag motion to fit the template. The zigzag lines should be touching. Pipe the tree trunk.

3 Pipe the base container using a no. 1 piping tube and full peak red icing.

4 With full peak green royal icing in a leaf bag (page 25), pipe a row of small leaves, starting at the bottom of the tree. Continue piping rows of leaves, working upwards and overlapping, until the base is covered.

Pressure Piping Figures

Many types of figures or animals, in various shapes and sizes, can be pressure piped using the techniques described below.

Materials

Royal icing

Equipment

Cellophane or waxed paper
Nos. 0 and 1 piping tubes (tips)
Piping bags
Artists' fine paintbrush

1 Secure a piece of lightly greased cellophane or waxed paper over the template of your choice (below).

2 First pipe the areas of the template that appear furthest away from you. Using a no. 1 piping tube and soft peak royal icing, pressure pipe the legs, arm and neck.

3 Using a no. 0 piping tube and soft peak royal icing, pressure pipe the face, then pipe the hair using a no. 1 tube and full peak icing, allowing the two areas to merge slightly. Pipe the hands in pull peak icing, using a zigzag movement to create the fingers.

4 Using a no. 0 tube and soft peak icing, pipe the shoes.

5 Pipe the sleeves and trousers with a no. 1 tube and soft peak icing, increasing the pressure to give shape to the arms and legs.

6 Use a no. 0 tube and soft peak royal icing to pipe the hat. Create a line in the brim with an artists' fine paintbrush.

7 Using a no. 1 piping tube and soft peak royal icing, pipe the jacket, skirt, etc., piping in the direction of the folds to achieve a fabric effect.

Tip

To add depth to your figure, pipe a 'matchstick' figure first and then pipe the clothes over the top.

Note

In the photographs below, the blue icing is used to identify the areas being piped at each stage.

Three-tier Wedding Cake

For the more experienced cake decorator, this romantic cake is adorned with pressure piped roses, figures and classic linework.

Materials

30x13cm (12x5 inch), 23x10cm (9x4 inch), 18x6cm (7x2½ inch) deep fruit cakes (see Note on page 34)
10kg (20lb) almond paste (marzipan)
8kg (16lb) royal icing
Apricot glaze
40cm (16 inch) chamfered cake board
30cm (12 inch) chamfered cake board
Three 20cm (8 inch) round cake drums
60g (2oz) green pastillage
White vegetable fat (shortening)
Edible glue

Equipment

Nos. 1, 2, 3, 42 piping tubes (tips)
Petal piping tube (tip)
Piping bags
Thin card or oval cutter
Craft knife or scalpel
Scriber
Balloon
Satay stick or dowel rod
Leaf piping bag (page 25)

Decorations

18 figures (page 32)
252 assorted roses (page 23) for bottom tier
120 small roses and rose buds for middle tier
48 miniature roses and rose buds for top tier

Preparation

1 Brush the cakes with apricot glaze and coat with almond paste, using the separate top and sides technique. Apply three coats of white royal icing to the cakes and chamfered boards, allowing each coat to dry before applying the next.

2 To make the plinth between the bottom and middle tiers, stick the three cake drums together. Coat the outside with three coats of royal icing, allowing each coat to dry before applying the next.

3 Scrape off any take-off marks with a small sharp knife. Secure the cakes to the chamfered boards using royal icing. Using full peak royal icing, fill in any gaps around the base edges of the cakes. Allow to dry.

Gazebo

4 Using the templates on page 48, prepare at least six run-out side pieces for the gazebo for the top tier. (Make spares in case of breakages.) Make at least six flange pieces and at least one run-out disc for the top. Leave to dry.

5 To make the top of the gazebo, carefully insert a satay stick or dowel rod into a partially aerated balloon, and grease the balloon with white vegetable fat. Pipe close filigree work on the balloon and leave overnight to dry.

6 Gently heat the balloon with a hair drier to melt the fat, then carefully deflate the balloon, leaving a lace top.

Bottom tier

7 Cut a strip of greaseproof paper the height and circumference of the side of the cake. Fold into 12 equal sections and cut a scalloped bottom edge with three scallops to each section. Secure around the cake.

8 Using nos. 3, 2 and 1 piping tubes and soft peak royal icing, pipe graduated linework around the scalloped template. Remove the template and repeat the graduated linework on the chamfered board.

9 Using nos. 42, 2 and 1 piping tubes, pressure pipe a 'C' scroll border around the top edge of the cake.

10 Roll out the pastillage thinly on a non-stick board. Trace the plaque template on page 48, transfer to thin card, and use to cut out 12 oval pastillage plaques. Secure to the cake with edible glue while the pastillage is still soft. Secure a piped figure on each plaque using soft peak royal icing.

11 Secure roses in bunches around the base of the cake, finishing with leaves piped using a leaf bag. Decorate the top of each plaque with a rose and two rose buds.

12 Pressure pipe diagonal lines around the outside of the plinth using a no. 2 piping tube and full peak royal icing.

Middle tier

13 Repeat steps 7, 8 and 9, opposite.

14 Attach garlands of piped roses above the linework on the side of the middle tier, using a leaf bag and full peak royal icing. Add small leaves.

Top tier

15 Trace and cut out the hexagon template on page 48. Place on top of the middle tier. Pipe around the outline of the hexagon, using a no. 2 piping tube and full peak royal icing, and allow to dry.

16 Carefully position six figures on the sides of the top tier cake. Pipe patches of grass around the figures. Place the cake in the centre of the middle tier.

17 Secure garlands of miniature roses to six run-out side panels. Using the piped hexagonal line as a guide, begin assembling the side panels to form the gazebo, ensuring the figures on the cake are visible through the panels. Attach flange pieces at the joins.

18 Secure the run-out disc on top of the gazebo with soft peak royal icing. Attach a garland of roses to the disc, adding leaves as before.

19 Pipe pressure piping consistency royal icing around the base of the lace dome and stick to the disc. Attach a miniature rose bud at each corner of the gazebo.

Note

We made the cake for the top tier in a clean rice pudding can. Line with greaseproof paper, fill with about 750g (1½ lb) rich fruit cake mixture (batter) and bake for about 1 hour.

Cherubs

These angelic little figures can be used as alternative motifs for the wedding cake (page 33) or as a side design for the heart-shaped cake (page 38). Alternatively, link them together with garlands of roses on a decorative plaque.

1 Secure a piece of lightly greased cellophane or waxed paper over the template on page 37. Starting with the area furthest away, use a no. 0 piping tube (tip) and full peak royal icing to pressure pipe loops to form the wings (as for birds, page 7). Pipe the back leg at the same time, using soft peak icing.

2 With a no. 1 tube and soft peak royal icing, pipe the neck and front leg, increasing pressure to shape the knee and calf. Pipe the face using the same icing.

3 With a no. 0 tube and full peak icing, pipe the hair, allowing it to merge slightly with the face.

4 Pipe the arms with a no. 1 tube and soft peak icing, increasing pressure at the elbows to give shape. Pipe the hands with a no. 0 tube and full peak icing, using a zigzag movement to create the fingers.

5 Pipe the body with a no. 1 tube and soft peak icing, increasing pressure to add detail, and agitating the icing with the tube, if necessary, to encourage a smooth finish.

6 To complete, pipe the drape across the cherub's body with a no. 0 tube and full peak icing. Use a dampened fine artists' paintbrush, if necessary, to create a drape effect.

Note

Blue icing has been used in the photograph below to identify the area being piped at each stage.

Cherub Plaque

1 Colour sugarpaste (rolled fondant) blue and use to coat a small rectangular board. Emboss the edge with an embossing tool.

2 Pipe a selection of cherubs from the designs below, and allow to dry. Attach the cherubs to the plaque with soft peak icing.

3 Using a no. 1 piping tube (tip) and soft peak green icing, secure swags of miniature roses and rose buds (page 24) to the plaque. To complete, pipe small green shells to represent leaves.

Ballerina 21st Cake

Perfect as it is for anyone interested in ballet, this cake can be made suitable for many other occasions simply by changing the colours and the motifs used.

Materials

25cm (10 inch) heart-shaped rich fruit cake
30cm (12 inch) heart-shaped cake board
1.5kg (3lb) almond paste (marzipan)
Apricot glaze
1kg (2lb) royal icing
Pink and yellow food colouring

Equipment

Cellophane or waxed paper
Nos. 1 and 2 piping tubes (tips)
Piping bags
Scriber
Non-slip mat

Decorations

11 daisies (page 21)
Ballet shoes (page 40)
2 ballerinas (page 40)

Preparation

1 Cut the cake so that the top slants towards the front (its pointed end). Brush with apricot glaze and coat with almond paste using the separate top and sides technique. Allow to dry for three days.

2 Apply white royal icing to the cake and board in three coats (or until a smooth finish is achieved), allowing each coat to dry before applying the next. Scrape down any take-off marks using a small sharp knife.

3 Secure the cake to the board with royal icing. Using full peak royal icing, fill in any gaps between the cake and the board. Allow to dry.

4 Secure a piece of lightly greased cellophane or waxed paper over the '21' template on page 48. Using a no. 1 piping tube and soft peak pink royal icing, pipe around the outlines, then fill in with pressure piping consistency royal icing of the same colour, agitating the icing gently with the tube to create a bold run-out finish. Leave to dry completely.

Oriental stringwork

5 Make a greaseproof paper template the height and circumference of the cake, cutting the top edge at an angle to match the sloping cake. Using a pencil, divide the bottom edge of the template into equal sections of approximately 3cm (1½ inches) each, depending on the size of the cake. Make corresponding marks along the top.

6 Wrap the template around the cake and mark the sections, top and bottom, on the icing with a scriber.

7 Pressure pipe bulbs at each mark using a no. 1 piping tube and soft peak white royal icing, taking care not to leave peaks. Using a no. 1 tube and full peak yellow icing, drop loops from each alternate bulb to the next.

8 Turn the cake upside-down on a non-slip mat, and pipe a second row of loops around the top and bottom of the cake. Repeat the technique in white to form a second layer of stringwork.

Decorations

9 Secure three groups of three daisies and two single daisies around the side of the cake. Attach the ballet shoes and bows to the front.

10 Secure the run-out numbers to the top of the cake with soft peak royal icing, then attach the ballerinas. Attach the piped tutus separately, then finish by piping ribbons on the ballet shoes with a no. 2 piping tube and soft peak white icing.

Ballerina

The technique used to create the ballerina off-pieces is a little different. The relief in the icing is achieved by piping 'padding' where needed. When dry, a second layer of icing is applied.

1 ▷ Secure a piece of lightly greased cellophane or waxed paper over the template on page 46. Using a no. 2 piping tube (tip) and full peak royal icing, first pipe the ballerina's tutu. Using a dampened paintbrush, brush embroider the icing up to create the appearance of folds in the fabric. Allow to dry.

2 ▷ Secure cellophane or waxed paper over the figure template and pipe the cheek, crown of the head, thigh and calf, keeping the icing just inside the template lines. (This will be the padding.)

3 ▷ Pipe the figure, beginning with the areas that appear furthest away. Pipe the back of the tutu first, using

brush embroidery to create folds. Next pipe the right arm, back leg, neck and shoulder, using run-out consistency flesh-coloured royal icing. The face and head are piped over the dry padding; this will give shape and definition.

4 ▷ After piping each part of the figure, allow the icing to dry long enough to form a crust before progressing to the next stage. When finished, allow to dry completely under a warm lamp. This will help to achieve a smooth, shiny surface.

5 ▷ Highlight contours by painting shading to the eotard and shoes. Paint the hair and face, using an artists' fine paintbrush and liquid food colours. Keep the brush quite dry to avoid dissolving the surface sugar.

Ballet Shoes

1 ▷ Secure a piece of lightly greased cellophane or waxed paper over the template below. Using a no. 1 piping tube (tip) and soft peak white royal icing, pipe two ovals for the soles.

2 ▷ Using a no. 1 piping tube and soft peak lemon icing, pipe the shoes. Allow to dry.

3 ▷ Make two bows as for the Rattle on page 15.

Teddy Birthday Cake

Decorated with teddy motifs and run-out bubbles, this is a delightful birthday cake for any young child.

Materials

Fruit cake baked in an upside-down number-two-shaped cake frame
Oblong cake board
1kg (2lb) almond paste (marzipan)
1.25kg (2½lb) white sugarpaste (rolled fondant)
Apricot glaze
500g (1lb) royal icing
Pink and blue edible lustre powders

Equipment

Cellophane or waxed paper
Soft dusting brush
No. 2 piping tube (tip)
Piping bags
Tracing paper
Thin card

Decorations

17 bears (page 42)

Preparation

1 Brush the cake with apricot glaze and cover with almond paste. Leave to dry for three days.

2 Coat the cake and board separately with sugarpaste. Allow to dry for three days.

3 Secure cellophane or waxed paper over the templates on page 47 and run out 14 various-sized white bubbles. Leave to dry. Dust with pink or blue edible lustre.

4 Carefully slide the cake on to the coated board. Using full peak royal icing, fill in any gaps around the bottom of the cake. Using a no. 2 tube and full peak royal icing, pressure pipe a line of small shells around the base of the cake.

Bubbles and bears

5 Trace the bubble templates on page 47, transfer to thin card and cut out. Place the card circles on the cake top, sides and board, where required, and dust with pink and blue lustre powders, brushing from the card templates on to the cake, and taking care each time to keep the area under the template free of colour.

6 Secure the run-out bubbles and bears at random on the top, sides and board, using a no. 1 piping tube and full peak royal icing.

41

Bears

The various areas are pressure piped in a slightly different sequence for each bear, depending on the bear's pose. Always begin with the area that appears furthest away.

1 Secure a piece of cellophane or waxed paper over a template. Using a no. 2 piping tube (tip) and soft peak cream/brown royal icing, pressure pipe the ears and body, agitating the icing with the tube to create a smooth surface. Pipe the head in the same way.

2 Pipe a bulb for each leg, then pipe a second layer of bulbs for the feet.

3 Pipe a bulb for the muzzle and small scrolls for the arms. Lastly, pipe a small black bulb for the nose.

4 When dry, airbrush, if liked, to create a fur effect. Complete by painting in facial features, piping on bow ties, etc.

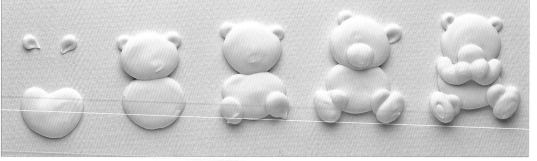

Pressure Piping Animals

These pressure piped '3D' animals are great for children's parties as they can be piped directly on to sweets or candies and then placed on small cakes.

Materials

Royal icing
Assorted food colourings
Assorted sweets and candies, e.g.
round mints, sugar-coated chocolate mini-eggs, large sugar-coated chocolate discs

Equipment

Piping bags
Cellophane or waxed paper
Nos. 0, 1, 2 and 5 piping tubes
(tips)

Faces

1 Pressure pipe round and oval bulbs in a variety of pale colours (see Features), using a no. 1 piping tube and run-out consistency royal icing, on to cellophane or waxed paper. Dry.

Bodies

2 Select a sweet, candy or mini-egg and attach to a sheet of cellophane or waxed paper with a small bulb of soft peak icing.

3 Pressure pipe the legs, arms and tails on to the sweets, using shells and bulbs to form the shapes. Different poses give character to the animals.

Features

4 The features are piped on to the dried run-out bulbs.

Elephant Choose a round, grey run-out disc. Using a no. 2 piping tube and soft peak grey royal icing, pipe two 'C' scrolls for the ears, then pipe a textured trunk. Use a no. 1 tube and full peak white icing for the eyes, finishing with a small black dot for the pupils, piped with a no. 0 tube.

Cow Attach a white run-out oval to a black run-out circle, then pipe on the features using a no. 1 tube and full peak black and white icing.

Dog Attach a brown run-out circle to a beige oval. Using a no. 5 piping tube and full peak brown icing, pressure pipe two scrolls for the ears. The features are piped in the same way as for the cow, above.

Pig Using a no. 1 piping tube and full peak pink icing, pressure pipe two shells for the mouth on to a round pink run-out disc. Draw a dampened artists' paintbrush through the shells to create a smile. With the same tube, pipe a large bulb for the nose. Pipe the ears using a leaf bag (page 25).

Rabbit Using a no. 1 tube and full peak light brown icing, pipe two shells for the ears on to cellophane or waxed paper, pushing the tube in and pulling down the icing for the ear holes. Leave to dry. Using a no. 1 tube and soft peak white icing, pipe two shells for cheeks on to a light brown run-out disc. Pipe a small bulb for the nose, using a no. 1 tube and soft peak black icing. Attach the ears.

Panda Starting with a white run-out bulb, pressure pipe two shells for the ears using a no. 1 tube and full peak black icing. For the eyes, form a heart shape by piping two black shells. Pipe a large bulb in full peak white icing for the nose, finished with a small black bulb.

Lion Using a no. 5 piping tube and full peak brown icing, pressure pipe small shells around a beige run-out disc. Pipe three shells coming forward at the top. Pipe the cheeks, eyes and nose as for the rabbit, above.

Finishing

5 Once the heads are dry, pipe a large bulb of icing on to each body and position the heads while the icing is still soft.

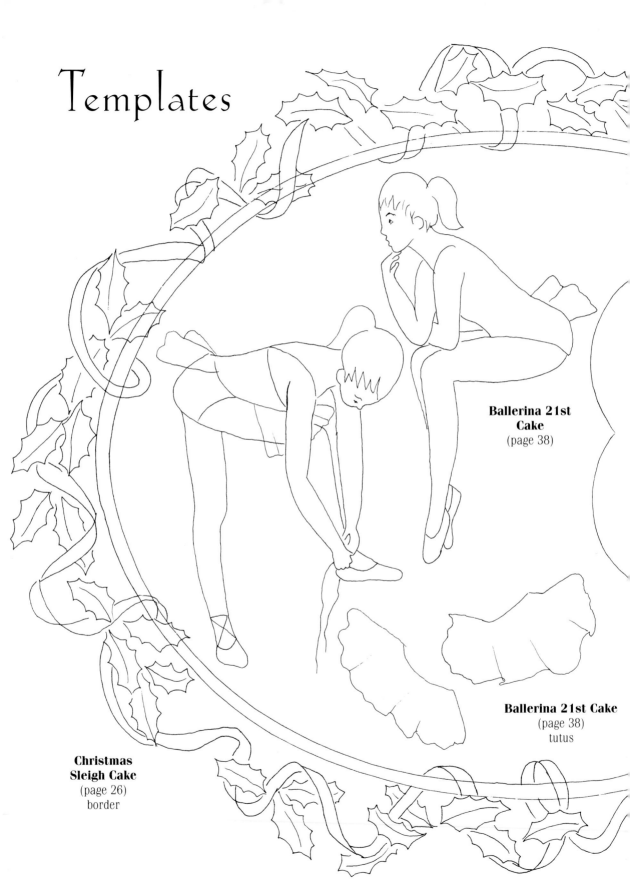

Templates

Ballerina 21st Cake
(page 38)

Ballerina 21st Cake
(page 38)
tutus

**Christmas
Sleigh Cake**
(page 26)
border

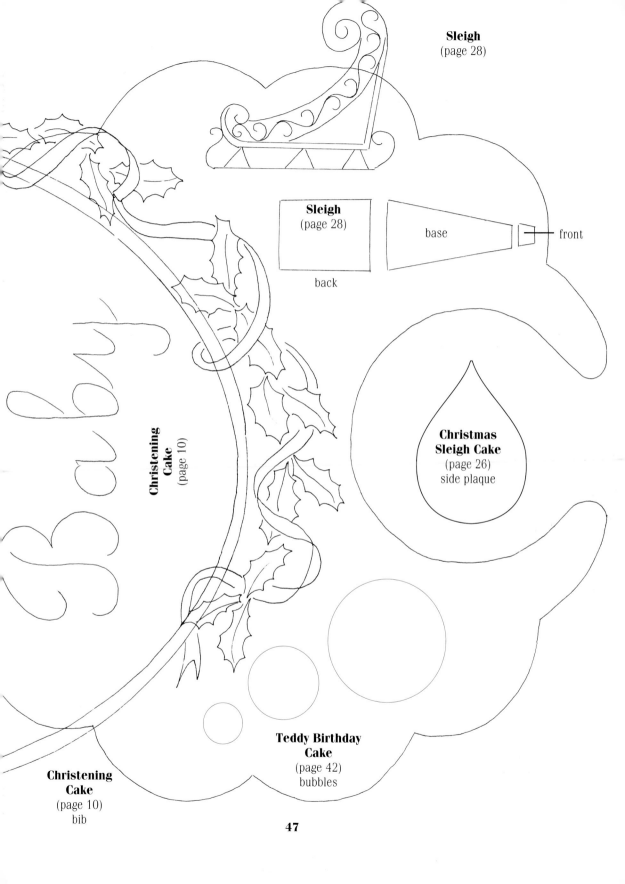

Sleigh
(page 28)

Sleigh
(page 28)

base

back

front

Baby

Christening Cake
(page 10)

Christmas Sleigh Cake
(page 26)
side plaque

Teddy Birthday Cake
(page 42)
bubbles

Christening Cake
(page 10)
bib

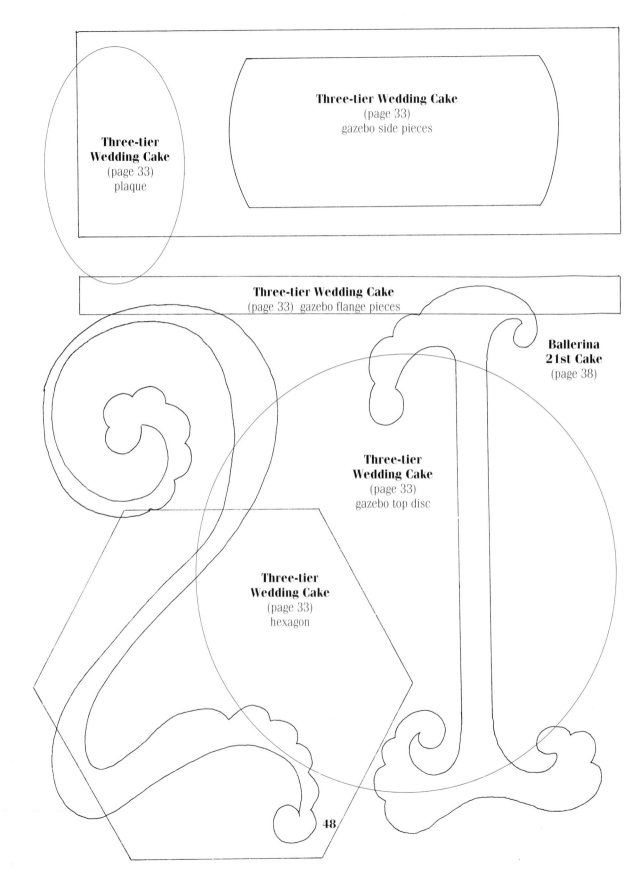

Three-tier Wedding Cake
(page 33)
plaque

Three-tier Wedding Cake
(page 33)
gazebo side pieces

Three-tier Wedding Cake
(page 33) gazebo flange pieces

**Ballerina
21st Cake**
(page 38)

**Three-tier
Wedding Cake**
(page 33)
gazebo top disc

**Three-tier
Wedding Cake**
(page 33)
hexagon